FINISHING LINE PRESS
www.finishinglinepress.com

Seminomad Prayer Termite

poems by

M. Jeanne Skvarla

Finishing Line Press
Georgetown, Kentucky

Seminomad Prayer Termite

ISBN 978-1-63534-150-8 First Edition

ACKNOWLEDGMENTS

Grateful acknowledgement is made to the following publications in which these poems, some in earlier versions, first appeared: "Instructions for the Anxious," "Meditation in the Grove of the Thinking Trees," "The Patient," "Moroccan Hash," "Once I was Chased Out of Galveston Bay," "I needed to become more," *Poetry East;* "Neither Here Nor There," "Because it's supposed to be spring," "When I came to," "Nightwatch," *College English;* "Some Degree of Shameful Relief," *Rattle.*

Publisher: Leah Maines

Editor: Christen Kincaid

Cover Art: Al Benas

Author Photo: Al Benas

Cover Design: Elizabeth Maines McCleavy

Printed in the USA on acid-free paper.
Order online: www.finishinglinepress.com
also available on amazon.com

Author inquiries and mail orders:
Finishing Line Press
P. O. Box 1626
Georgetown, Kentucky 40324
U. S. A.

Table of Contents

For my mother, Donna

Because it's supposed to be spring,

treeroots brush the hair
from the foreheads
of the thawing dead.
You think *so what?*
when you see tennis shoes
hanging from telephone lines;
so far you've come through
every close call
unscathed. You're walking,
hating the way perverts
look like congressmen
these days, thinking
there must be something left.
Underground, you like the sound
of T-tokens in the turnstiles,
as you wait for the train
that will take you home,
back to your two-eyed mother,
the one who really loves you.

When I came to,

it was later than I thought.

A tiny person was sleeping on my arm
like a still blue answer.

In a different room,
behind a half-open doorway,

another one sat on his knees
transcribing what the farmhouse said.
I couldn't quite make out the words.

Later, he slept at the top
of a wooden staircase,
the sunbeams shifting across his back.

I went home to my bird,
to catch up on the war;

after that, it was a long time
before anything happened.

When the World Was Their Clam

It was a great big house,
with two white chimneys;

yesterday someone knocked
on one of them.

The surrounding lawn was the dying
lawn of the one-legged crow,

and the mimosa picked its way
around the place, passing

the window of the cross-dressed
darlings of the bible belt.

Inside the house, a clock chimed
eight times at noon,

and the cooling sex partner
gently reassembled

her many selves.

Nightwatch

Today you rode
an abandoned bicycle
through an empty place
for hours, hoping to wear
yourself out, but now
it's evening and you're
not worn out, not yet.
You don't know what it is,
but people seem to be
dropping like flies these days,
bodies coming apart
in the bathwater,
thoughts going the way
of misplaced earrings;
you find it all so unsettling,
but these are the things
you think about.
What you really want
is a better bedtime story
and someone to tell it.
You want it all to be simple,
but it never really is;
intrepid insomniac,
unaccompanied,
still holding tightly
to your ticket for sleep.

Neither Here Nor There

Kris put a pawnshop special
in her mouth
one morning,
and didn't chicken out.
The bullet
is still in her head,
in the place
where some wiseacre
thought
must have stopped it.

Self-Portrait with Streets at Age 25

I like the laughing camel
smoking cigarettes
on the downtown billboards
as I traipse down Lincoln Boulevard
like a groggy whore on a hot afternoon,
thinking that someday the famous floating soap
will sink and we'll all be so disappointed.
I still marvel at the birds, though,
and the fact that they can fly, which is
kind of amazing. And relatively speaking,
it's fortunate how few of us go nuts
in post offices and supermarkets,
given the heat, the traffic,
the numbers of unruly children.

Just now, the cops whiz by: someone
has done something bad.
I light my cigarette
from a burning building,
and keep my feet moving
toward a late night taco stand
where I imagine romance,
protest, and consider joining a cause;
cures, fund-raisers, endless marching:

Stepstools for the short.
Leg Room for the tall.

Moroccan Hash

An extended search
for an outrageous earring.
Ingmar Bergman this,
and Ingmar Bergman that.
A Swedish acupuncturist
and a small Texan tourist
watch the moon spin
through a window
of the Royal Dublin Hotel.

I needed to become more

lifelike, move around a little,
talk to people. *How about a walk*
through the mouse garden?
I asked my self. Nothing.
Outside the window
an oak tree emptied its children
like a horrible twisting Jesus.
Maybe what I needed was a new kind of sky.
How 'bout a game of cards, then?
I asked. *Empress of India?*
House on the Hill? Forty Thieves?
Still nothing. *C'mon,* I said,
I'll let you win. Really. I will.
A turnip began dancing
in a corner of the dark kitchen.
The lettuce froze on the drainboard.
I knew I had to become more real.
Hey, I said, are you listening?
...are you there...are you?

Love Poem

Things are still groovy
at the Los Doñas apartments,
across from Walter Mitty's
where they've got
girls girls girls
and blue-faced men
tossing each other
in and out of the bar all night.
It's a tiny place in Oklahoma
and we are the lovers
in this screwball comedy
of leaky heaters, barsmoke,
and broken jaws,
sleeping like spoons
on a springless Murphy.
You are the Mexican chef
behind my eyeballs,
your bony arms
firing up the enchiladas.
I love you.

Once I was Chased Out of Galveston Bay

The thing may still be after me,
I don't know, I never looked back.
Later, when I was fourteen,
I said I'd give a guy named Tracey Stewart
fifty bucks to eat the thing
in the dissecting dish.
He did (he lived), and I didn't.
Later on in this same lifetime,
I fell off a horse and saw stars.
Incredible, isn't it? These days
I pass my time strung out on soda-pop
and humming old cowboy tunes,
which doesn't seem unusual to me.
I have painted ladies in my backyard,
a mutt called Moses at my feet,
and a gun, a hundred-dollar gun,
which is not so important anymore,
not really, since there's nothing to shoot.
And though I'm way too young for this,
(I'm much too young, I know it),
I ask myself time and time again,
every day I ask myself,
I say, *hmmm…what do I do now?*
and sometimes, something answers.

A Distant Symphony

The hedge crept down the drive.
You looked at your watch;
it was late, a moonless night,
the stars like so many broken teeth.
Soft red syllables everywhere;
they could never,
never be properly arranged.
Oath, excuse, explanation....
After all, what was there,
what was there, really, to say?
3:00 a.m. went by on crutches,
crickets did what they could.
What was it you expected?
At least someone loved you.

Instructions for the Anxious

Listen to the radio pirate playing his songs.
Listen in your dim kitchen,
standing at the sink scraping soupcans,
listen as you wander city streets,
transistor radio pressed to your ear.
Forget the loneliness, and what it may do to you
(perhaps it will make you beautiful).
Think instead of flowers in a garden:
geranium, petunia, begonia,
awkward names for awkward plants,
but in time you will care for them more
than the wild ones you love so much
(after all, someone had to think to put them there).
Things will change, they always do,
and when severed hands come crawling toward you
to begin the work on the knots in your back
you'll know you are ready
for a long, cryonic rest. Let well-wishers
wish you well, then you are free to go.
Like some stars, you may go for weeks
without being seen; and like the stars,
you'll be small when viewed
with the naked eye
alone.

Ineluctable Madness

The tricycle-masters are out of town;
my love for them turns

as the turkey in the oven burns for nobody,
and tomatoes sit on the windowsill,

my artificial sisters, sniveling,
and soaking up sunshine.

It's the season of rusty nails now,
and the trees and things have buds,

but today I will not go out.
I no longer believe in sparrows,

and my interest in earthworms has waned.
The neighbor's neighbors bicycle by;

so many times I mistake them for ghosts.
The suns go up and down, up and down,

Dear God, I say, but I can't
find the words to finish—

it's hard to make small talk
with someone like that.

Nothing to do but think, I think,
my single-handed timepiece pounding,

and the things that keep me, boring,
snuggled inside my brain.

The Patient

You may eat whatever you
want, now, the doctor said,
just don't expect to feel well
afterward. "Bitch...."
said the sailors in my submarine heart
as I laughed, a low, secret,
stay-awake laugh, as if she were
holding a rubber chicken
or wearing wax lips,
and I made my way to the pharmacy
to get my prescription steak,
then limped back home, pressing it
gently against my one black eye,
and gently against the other.
Someday I'll feel better all over,
I'm sure of it, and perhaps
my mood will improve as well.
We scheduled my next appointment
in the supermarket, then changed it
to the mall, or Venice, or Paris.
This was not my idea. However,
I have my reservations.
For this reason, I am compelled
to include her name here. It was
Goldstein, M.D., and, as far as I know,
it still is.

The Sex Shop

                    was blinking quietly
in the failing light.

Leaves unhooked themselves
from the candleberry branches;

the wind carried them off
like little blasphemies.

You felt the mummies stir inside you,
and knew it was evening again.

Thinking of nightcaps, forecasts,
and the nameless thing you believe in,

you couldn't see the gigantic
traveling lies bunched by the curb.

The runaway who had come a million miles
saw them, and tossed his sputtering bombs.

When you heard the tiny explosions,
one of your hearts went out to him.

Sirens, fever, the conspiracy
of bricks and you, reckless,

alone in your grimy digs,
you haven't cried for a week;

you must be happy.

Meditation in the Grove of the Thinking Trees

I hardly know where to begin.
Each morning I'm shocked into life
at the sight of the Thinking Trees—
symmetrical, perfect, and no two the same.
Each one true to itself and itself alone.
Traveling by wheelbarrow,
you'll need a fearless companion
and a half-day to reach them
(though the former is difficult to come by,
and therefore not really required).
Oh, there are faster and easier ways
to go, yes, but none so fulfilling
as this, the most difficult way.
Once arrived, rest your feet
on the bragging boulders of boredom.
Lay down your peashooter, call
off your cousins, and slurp your soup,
the Dogcatcher Stew, with the fabulous
unbagged mutts of this planet Earth.
And don't look now (don't look),
but here comes your enemy,
your favorite one, filthy, seething
and pissed, he's heading your way:
don't smile, don't smile.

Some Degree of Shameful Relief

It should not have been as hilarious as it was
when the pallbearers almost dropped you;
I just kept thinking *thank God the unbearable*
bellyache is over. Your graffiti bloodsplatter
pattern suggested a .357 to the mouth;
we confirmed this with our mops and sponges.
I put my finger in the hole in the wall
where the bullet passed through,
having passed through you first.
I imagine it's still in orbit somewhere,
and will eventually pierce an alien being
whose body will slap down to earth
some lovely summer Sunday like today.
But your fifteen minutes were fantastic!
They glued your noggin back together
like a bone china crackle finish wig head!
Father Fluchet made an exception for you
(lucky you!) and everyone sobbed and said *poor you!*
Church ladies bucketlined casseroles in and out
of the house for three whole days, and those who had eaten
your jalapeño lasagna were cooler for the day
than those who had not when the eulogist
praised it at the service. After we buried you,
I took the weed your friends left on your grave
and smoked it out on Thunderbird dam.
And there, amid the grackles and bass boats,
I tried like heck to believe in the enormous, people-eating
freshwater octopus that some say roams
these dirty waters. But what I decided instead
was that some people just never really do
learn how to swim.

A Few Haiku

Morning Poem

Sunrise on Red Creek;
a woman rows a red skull,
singing with the loons.

* * *

Haiku Number Something

Long rainy spring day
the roof rats in the attic
eating baseball cards.

* * *

Dead Presidents (Lettuce)

Clams, cabbage and bread—
—the live rate of currency
(cheddar Benjamin).

Dr. Friedman

Cora says the universities are full of fascists anymore,
and that she doesn't fit in and that I wouldn't either.
She says she is an automaton, a teacher borg.
She is weeding Moonbeam's grave as she tells me this.
She's bitter, she admits it, and seems to be aging strangely.
We talk for a while, but I don't say much that's right,
and then she says she has to go: she's going shopping
to buy herself a present, something nice, from her husband Jon.

Dave Has Been Struck by Lightning Twice

To be struck by lightning and survive
is quite a thing; to have this happen twice
is to be really singled out by God.
This is why I pay such close attention
to what my friend Dave says and does,
even though his hair offends me
and he often seems to make no sense at all.

Off the Hook

The other day Jeff sent an e-mail that said, look, look at this
and what did I think. I looked and I thought he was probably right,
that this was the John S. we'd been worried about, the one
we'd grown up with and had lost track of, and it was so good,
such a relief to find that he was already dead and buried
in in Greenville Texas, and not sitting on death row in Indiana
after all, as we'd mistakenly believed, for the past two years.

Antipode

From Santiago, Chile, to Xi'an, China;
from Santa Rosa, Argentina, to Jinan.
Tunnel, man, wherever. Just get yourself
elsewhere. The Kodak's busted
and the canaries are wicked wised up
anymore. Sorry about that. Still, we must
connect. An unstoppable digging contraption
roars back to life. (It roars.) A field
of orange dandelions blooming on the floor
of the Indian Ocean is one idea
of a likely destination. We hope.
We work hard. My cupped hand
resting in the dirt, a backhoe on its terrible
ugly knuckles. From down here,
I can sense the sunset, and the arrival
of the stars, and then the silence,
and finally the stones themselves,
crying out from the earth.

Navigational Patterns (A Love Sonnet)

I splashdown at our waypoint meeting place
with gyroscopic heart. My azimuth
is all fucked up, and I can't calculate
the change. It's like a game of blindman's bluff,

a game of tag in which I trip and move
by senses other than plain sight. (Inside
the kennels of my dizzy brain, a slew
of skinny mutt pups sniffs and sniffs and whines

then points me down the safest path.) And so
it goes, here in our secret land: the stuff
of us, magnetic North, the maps unfold,
the suns and moons our guides. But still, it's tough

at times to tell the lightening bugs from stars,
which makes it hard to travel very far.

Extraordinary Day

To awaken, disempowered, from the dream
of telekinesis. Failing even to mind-budge
the fluff from a dandelion gone to seed.
It's a happy thing, or an almost happy thing
to wish away the morning fog, within which
Eastern commas work like mad to disambiguate
the day. It's ordinary. (It's extraordinary.)
Then a street-cleaning pelican
bumps a crate of perfectly-packed
tetrahedral tomatoes from the bed
of a clattering farm truck. (We'd waited
so long for these!) And someone finds
a magpie's nest brimming with
magnificent, unmatched earrings!
It's a thing though, it's quite a thing
as the sun begins to sink, to watch
the twisted playground slide
dispensing children from the roiling pink:
once arrived, they pause to empty rainwater
from their small green galoshes,
and then are completely consumed
by the wild roadside tiger lilies.

Spontaneous Combustion

The magnifying glass inspection of
a Spanish fly that caused the farmer's son
to set the barn on fire by accident
made everybody nod and blame to the hay
(brought in before it dried). They said *I told*
you so, and, *these things happen now and then,*
as if the sudden breaking into flame
were normal and ok. As if it were
another humdrum part of life. And when
the sky grew dark with thunderheads, they all
said *must be gonna rain* and left for home.
And then the cattle-killing hail began
to fall; the farmer's son believed it looked
like all the baseballs ever slugged or thrown
into the summer sun returning home.
He never told a single living soul.

Five Percent

By my estimation, you've stuck yourself
over one hundred and seventeen
thousand times. And it all goes so perfectly
(meaning there are fields of okra in your eyes).
It is some kind of miracle or not, then; it appears
there is more to life than luck after all.
(In case of emergency, though, please crack open
an ice-cold king Coke.) I, of course, did not understand
for the longest time, mistakenly imagining
the Islets of Langerhans as a rocky cluster
off the coast of Maine, where pharmaceutical cattle
stood around all day, not making insulin
instead of making milk. You said they said with luck
you might see forty. (By fifty you'd buried two kids.)
You said *what a thing to say to a mother.* I thought
what a thing for a child to hear. We knew that
no one knew for sure, but still. All I knew for sure
was this: you did not become a cowgirl after all.
When you left for college, your mother threw out
your stamp collection. Then you married a man
who turned out not to be the man you married.
(You said this was just life.) You once tried the papergirl's
new moped and drove it into the fence by accident.
In those days, it was all just flabbergasting.
There were freight trains in the wind. Sometimes
it rained sideways, and sometimes it rained mulberries.
The important thing was that for a short time
we all had such fabulous purple footprints.
There was a centurion friend who lived at the end
of a red dirt road lined with wild iris; she swore by goat's milk
and beets. You say you want to move the baby's grave.
You say you are one of the five percent you swore
you would be. *Everybody dies*, you cheerfully remark
every so often, as if this were perfectly normal.

Among other things,

thanks for the flocks of sheep
who look like goats
and sound like children
pretending they are sheep
that look like goats
and for the shepherds
who must walk with them
for so many kilometers
every day so the ricotta
will turn out right
thanks for the kilo of tomatoes
in the rope bag and for the
roadside cactus paddles thanks
for the fennel the lotus
the lettuce the prickly pear
the bumpy bus and for
the two deaf boys sitting
in the back whose hands
and fingers flutter
like pale birds talking
about ordinary things
no one else can understand.

Lucky

The rag doll's emergency backup eyeball
is my vegetable ivory lucky button
from which I draw gumption and giddy up.
Lucky, having been harvested from the rain-forests
of Ecuador, having been cut and polished
in a secret process in a Rochester, NY factory
just before the turn of the century (the last
and more famous one, not this most recent
one (turn, that is, of the century)), but anyway,
having fallen off an overcoat from a secondhand store,
having endured a legacy of human enterprise,
and having saved some lucky African elephants
along the way. Too bad there's nothing to see,
cycloptically speaking, from the inside of a pocket,
just a few old seams in the blinking darkness, curled
around some ragged idea or other. So then one day
comes along the little woolen one-eyed head
with its body flapping around beneath it.
It's inevitable, really, and what is there to do,
what can I do, standing there all
two-dimensional-like, when the time comes
to give over the button, sacrifice the sacramental,
venture headlong into the fringe itself, wide-eyed
and unkissed, hanging on by a few faded time-worn threads;
it should not be this difficult, it should not be.

Jets and Crape Myrtle

There were jets and some brown rats and lots of crape myrtles.
There were jets like noisy darts tearing up the oceanside air.
There were brown rats living in the neatly-clipped back yards
(and also in the not-so-neatly clipped back yards). There were
crape myrtles, huge ones, which formed a canopy over many
of the back yards above which the noisy darts tore up
the oceanside air, and below which the brown rats lived.
There was a young man who practiced with his brand new
telekinetically-operated bionic hand (which fascinated
some people and grossed out others), by throwing darts
in the general direction of the brown rats. Of course, the jets
roared overhead, and the brown rats kept on being rats,
and the crape myrtle, which (incidentally) came in *Dynamite Red,*
Pink Velour, and *Twilight Purple*, lit up the false undersky
to acknowledge the half-assed, unsuccessful assault
on the unmaimed rats. The jets left a thermal signature
which attracted heat-seeking missals who arrived later
in the form worn-out banshees. The darts left a good,
old-fashioned cursive signature. The oceanside air
was punctuated briefly with a small tornado with tiny hips.
(The rats ran for cover.) Much of the crepe myrtle
had been trimmed and trained into erotic 3D puzzle presentations
(their sexy, flesh-colored branches so very much resembled
boneless human arms). Anyway, the good old-fashioned signature
was invisible and obsolete, and so the worn-out banshees
declared the small tornado king. And the crape myrtle,
did I mention how great life was beneath that crape myrtle dome?
And how about that fabulous telekinetic hand?

Mrs.

Having been born from your mother's mummy (enough to fuck up the best of us),

it was no surprise that you lived your life alone, wrapped up in silk
inside of your gin-scented home.

And having failed to metamorphose (in the way that we fail to metamorphose),
you gave up on your vestigial kisser (ineffectual noisemaker, useless
piehole),

having never developed an appetite for needles anyway. How your inoperable
antennae could not even sense the faintest pulse of *yeah, there are others
of us out here, too.*

Inglorious stump-legged cripple (with busted unflappable wings to boot), perhaps
you have already lived the one best moment allotted you:

ballooning in the breeze that one good day back in the day, in the heat of the
stinkeye sun, toward an evergreen homestead that suggested so much
(imagine: evergreen!);

the wind blew you where it wanted you (so it is with one borne of the wind),
then went on its way, no one knows where;

you went on to build your inconspicuous, pretty pinecone house in which you
lived equivocally, indistinguished, a fecked and feckless life.

Brass Goggles

Abandoning now at once and for good
the search for the kudzu-covered mooring mast
on which to dock my dirigible (what a jackass
I must look like through the quizzing glass of God,
having browsed his empty mind for hours). The point is.
The point is what? (Oh busted thrunge plate!)
Somewhere down there a man is whacking his way
through the imitation topiary, which grows, they say,
at a rate of one unfurling foot per day. But how lovely the aviation,
I mean the aviary, between hither and yon; one can't swing a dead cat
without smacking down delivery drones and their whifferous pizza payloads.
I say these things with some intimation of authority. As if I knew
a goddamned thing about the mind of God, or the kudzu future,
as if a functioning thrunge plate has ever existed, as if whifferous
were really a word, as if I were anything more than a heavily-ruffled orphan
desperate to get my wiggle on elsewhere.

Toxic Traffic Clusterfuck Province of Caserta

Think mis-sense, nonsense and frameshifts.
Think fucked-up mutant food chain.
The almond trees feeding on underground
rivers of nuclear effluvia forced up
through the green fuse of grapevines,
steaming crops of irradiated artichokes,
broad beans sizzling inside their sludge-pods.
The cancer vans roll out from the city
to cook the blood counts, to slam in
vinca alkaloids in poison shots
of pharmaceutical futility.
Even as the soil gas rises from the tilled earth
like the toxic ghosts of bodies left stewing
in the groundwater, acres of intracranial,
stellate hell-flowers bloom like gangbusters
in polluted mind fields, with no intention
other than immortality, and no real mission
to harm their hosts. Malignant, yet not malign,
they have no off-switch, no pre-programmed,
apoptotic plan like all other living cells
known to man; in other words, each one
urges on and on; procreant, radioactive,
perpetual life.

Candle Packing

For two lost years in steel-toed sneaks I sent
the candles out. The votives, tapers, tea
lights groovy with a cosmic, karmic bent.
I boxed up love; at first the gig was sweet.

I can't forget the twisted crazy way
the funnels full of packing peanuts fell
from ceiling nets above, to insulate
the waxy scented stuff my cartons held.

I moved through hazy petrochemic winds
of thick perfume and paraffin and dye.
It seeped into my skin; there was no end
to wheezing breath or burning, itching eyes.

It wasn't light that I was sending out,
just corporate gain, in polystyrene clouds.

Dime Store Wondertube Telescope

Peering through the pinhole
of my crumpled cardboard lens,
I watch the black holes dine
on dream variations of the disenchanted.
(Oh happy vegan shoestore lost to hooligan rule!)
(Oh empire of salty cheese ruined by embezzler mice!)
The hungry void is a crippled whore
who once loved to play with dolls.
Her story is a sea chanty sung by the comets;
how she longs to be kissed in the flares
of a great solar storm. Oh glitter of space junk,
oh dead weight of moonbeams, oh sniffer dogs sprawled
on the wizard blue lawn; death is an eggplant
that floats on the gloam, time is a plate with a crack.
Oh kibble of terry-cloth capes; oh faded hero mask,
oh silverware windchimes that rock my ossicles
with the sounds of incessant snacking.

The Secret of Life

It's one hot kiss that melts the snowman's cheek,
the gone assailant's footprints filling quick
with shadows from the bare and trembling trees,
the kiss itself a steaming cursive script

of un-cracked code. Or it's a hidden mode
of everlasting iteration, like
a Fibonacci fractal motherlode
of undiscovered information. I

suspect sometimes it's something else instead:
a disco pasta alphabet that churns
inside a cast iron pot (the boiling text
undone). And here's the bitch of all these words:

there is no kiss or code or secret soup,
there's just one unsolved algorithmic you.

Votives

—after Machado

High in the hills above Spoleto and Perugia,
up along the summits of Monte Acuto
and Monte Vettore, sixth century Umbrian shepherds once
guided their flocks up the transhumance routes
to the summer pastures, carrying with them
small bronze offerings to divinities.

Above those ancient valleys where
church bells still sound on Sundays,
they consecrated these human figures
in stone alcoves inside their sanctuaries.
Naked warriors with spears and shields
held high, and other empty-handed characters
with arms open wide in attitude of devotion and prayer.

Oblation of violence, oblation of adoration,
who knows which sacrifice a god prefers?

Here in the Museo Archeologico di Spoleto,
these votives appear a little off-balance;
faceless, disoriented, they've wandered
away from one another, with no ancient path
inside their clean glass case
on which to anchor their cleated feet.

All sanctuaries eventually rot. I carry my own
sacred offerings in a cavern of my heart,
season after season, year after year,
my own footprints, my only path.

Boy Flying a Raptor Kite in an Abandoned Ballfield

A boy flies his red-tailed hawk into the ash-filled air;
it's the only chickenhawk in Sicily, he's pretty sure
about that. He must like the way the smoke-scented sunshine
settles on the field; he must like the chain-link tapestry
of flowering weeds, and the intrepid turtle Owen,
who comes and goes though a hole in the fence
by the rundown dugout. Once in a while,
the paper bird of prey swoops and dives,
pulling at the end of the cotton kite string
as if it's come alive at the sight
of something delicious, something far beyond
what the boy can see or even begin to imagine.
But the boy, stedfast, holds the bird
for as long as he can, until finally it breaks away
and disappears in the direction of the Tyrrhenian Sea.
It soars past the Love Story nightclub, where
young American sailors go to unwind
with Ukrainian girls who pole dance
to pay off transit debts that will never go away.
It passes over the Lido Rossello by the Turkish Steps,
lousy with Sicilian bravado and flair,
and catches a Scirocco wind, gust of
hope, gust of death to so many African migrants.
But back at the base, the boy reels in
the extra kite string; I imagine he'll someday
wonder what's on the other side of that fence, anyway,
who carved the word *Owen* into the pond turtle's shell,
and understanding, suddenly, that *Owen* might not
really be that turtle's name after all.

—Sigonella Naval Air Station
Catania, Sicily, 2013

A Can of Ro*Tel and Some Velveeta Cheese

You did not even know you were sad you did not but every time you walked headfirst into that cold cold wind for some half time you time which no one could understand because why would anyone do that already there it was: the tears coming sideways out of your eyes and I shit you not freezing like gemstones to the sides of your head I swear if you'd wanted to and you didn't want to you could have picked them off and carried them around in a little drawstring bag the kind that pirates and small children and medieval people in picture books carry you could have kept them forever you could have been rich like that just as long as it always stayed winter and some kind of some kind of game was always going on

Love Poem with Orecchiette

We made orecchiette for hours that evening
listening to the night rooster's rant.

He kept singing *the Catanian stars*
are the same as anywhere else,

a work song that stoned us silly,
but we sang along in hysterical falsetto.

Your hair was a tuft of milk-vetch
blooming on the ash fields of Etna;

your eyes were lava lakes
glowing in the wine-lit kitchen.

There was no end to the dough, our
thumbprints, our warm neurotic kneading.

At dawn, you rode a red Pinarello
into the steaming sunrise;

I watched Etna blow smoke rings
toward the distant Ionian Sea.

The farmers were out burning their fields;
the sheep moved like soot on the the plain.

Hundreds of little ears remained,
drying in the morning heat,

filled with the lovesick murmur of us.

The Oldest Heart in the World

belongs to an ancient shrimp, who packed
his tiny shrimp-heart across the turbulent sea floor

of southwest China 520 million years ago,
who carried it on his shrimp-back, like an eighth-grader

with a book-bag rucksack inside of which
lived eons of undiscovered shrimp stories,

whose fossilized shrimp-shell showed nerve-maps
proving the distance from heart to brain

has always been an endless expanse of shrimp distance;
who proves that shrimp-time, for whatever reason,

has reverse-diversified the structure of shrimp hearts,
who rails that even when trapped, crushed, flattened,

forgotten, packed in shrimp-mud and petrified
in an environment inhospitable to shrimp growth

someone shrimpish will eventually find you, dust you off,
and gaze at you with innocent, shrimp-like love and wonder.

Don't Count Your Chickens Before They Hatch

Because some will be stolen by rats, snatched up by hawks, or swallowed by
snakes (this is the way that it's always been),

and some eggs (it's important to remember), are just bad to begin with
and won't ever hatch at all.

Some will be stepped on by accident by the hen keeper herself, alone and tipsy
in the springtime moonlight.

Some will have crack patterns indicating ominous events; their chicks will emerge
with backward feet and crumpled beaks (and these are the ones who will
break our hearts).

Many will simply disappear one day, and no one will notice until it's far too late
(*what happened?* we will say, *we don't understand what just happened).*

Half will be roosters, of course, who will need new homes, a difficult thing to find
on a good day, and most days are fair at best,

and many will walk away right after hatching; their footprints like tiny peace
signs in the dirt road leading to someplace else; there will be

so many of these, they'll be impossible to count.

Dadgum Dirt Road of Wandering Dogs

—after T.S. Eliot as Old Possum

There was one with a cracked tooth, and one with shattered eyes,
one who carried a stick, one who barked at sheep,
and one who spoke the language of the weeds.

There was one whose footprints were sewn to the dirt
by the many-hearted earthworms who sang hallelujah
as the old narcotic eye of God moved like the moon
through the trees.

There was one who'd bailed from a shelter-bound cruiser
while his master was taken to the morgue,
and another who carried a century of stars
in the soft blue hairs of her fur.

There was one who'd sniffed out bed bugs and bombs,
and another who could even climb trees.

There was one who'd stowed his bone maps
in a fragrant curl of the renegade wind;
another who suffered from sticker-burr pricks
in the black patent pads of his paws.

There was one forever chasing his tail,
like a grateful ghost unloosed
by chance percolations of the forest floor.

There was one who snacked on scarebabies,
one who smelled like a hash pipe,
and one who would howl at the dim city lights
until daisies rained from the sky.

Sometimes I forget to remember you,

little baby, untrapped earthling,
psychedelic sparrow lost in the sun.

Marfa light on my tilted horizon
whence your cushioned boomerang comes.

Once I joyrode four-hundred sleet-slicked miles
just to let the bottlerockets fly

from the hands of the crumbled angel
who guards your weedy grave.

I guess you know by now
the sound of the wind in space.

Moon thistle, invisible sister,
jigger of twinkling satellites;

this is my lunatic toast
to the small dancing shadow

of your singular,
five-hour life.

Bible Belt Rivalry (1980 or thereabouts)

Three Catholic kids
behind the bowling alley,
smoking a joint
rolled in a page
torn from the Protestant bible.

Visual Field Test

The drusen in your eyes are on your nerves;
like moviegoers in Miranda hats,
those extra actors in your theater,
bombastic dingbat silhouettes amassed

to block your line of sight. Irascible
spectactrix (hoodwinked watcher), patsied, duped
and tricked percipient; ostensible
reality informs your shaded truth.

But on the visual field at six o'clock
(some lone, empurpled shadows hanging out),
a peaceout pocks the unenlightened plot;
you wonder what the fuss is all about:

that blind spot's been there forty years or so—
—you never noticed—right beneath your nose.

Cub Scout Pack 66 Snack Drive for the Homeless Kids' After-School Tutoring Program

We brought some psychedelic cheese food twists
and bright orange peanut butter crackers; hauled
in small atomic, pizza-flavored fish,
and squishy, fruited polymeric globs

in boss, robotic shapes. *Cool beans!* the Big
Cheese said: *I see you let the boys pick out*
these things themselves; our kids will really dig
this stuff, as kids know best what kids like most.

Oh algebraic proof with tartrazine!
Indigotine geography! I guess
those kids will be okay eventually
or not. They'll trudge through time like all the rest

of us, and (hopefully) will someday find
beneath the toxic crust: a killer life.

Ferguson's Trestle

All anyone knows for sure about Ferguson
is that a hellbent vigilante mob

(a bastard rabble posse of the dirty deindividualized),
commandeered a locomotive from the Antonito yards

and drove it westbound to the trestle at mile 285.87,
where there was just enough height for him to hang

for a crime that no one these days much remembers:
maybe some kind of cattle-rustling-

horse-thieving-dynamiting-thing; maybe something
to do with a woman. Maybe

a burgled hope buried in an amethyst-silver vein
land claim. Whatever it was,

it was something that mined the comprehensive,
incomprehensible collective unrest

of the ripshit pissed off. I imagine Ferguson's toes
must have just cleared the sagebrush

(those unlit Navajo smudge shrubs); they must have
just cleared the wormwood (oh pale yellow flowers

of bitter absinthe), his shallow trestle a dusty decoration
bridging one sorry side of the endless chaparral

to the other. But what we know for sure
is next to nothing because this is all

the guidebook offers to passengers like me,
riding the tourist train that chuffs along

of the mapmaker's legend; I hear the melodious code

of whistlespeak; this train goes to places I never expected
not to visit (poor Ferguson) quite so soon.

the narrow gauge tracks. I study the cryptic script
of the mapmaker's legend; I hear the melodious code

of whistlespeak; this train goes to places I never expected
not to visit (poor Ferguson) quite so soon.

Dark Poem of the Ambivalent Bunn

In 1985 in Shortcake's Diner in Stillwater OK gigantically hungover Jeff and I sat scandalized in the back by the Bunn-O-Matic Coffee station on hearing our favorite waitress Jo (our Jo!) had just been arrested for participating in a snuff film ring or at least that's what the O'Colly newspaper claimed; in 1997 Pour-O-Matic technology was there as my partner and I sat inside the guards' room off the sally port in the the Hampton County House of Corrections in Ludlow MA while someone searched our ambulance for bombs while the man who had hung himself in his cell from a three foot high sink using a rope made from strips of his own shirt went ahead and died; in 2004 in the back room of Julius the Tailor's shop off of North Pleasant St. in Amherst MA the unbreakable globe-shaped carafe cast a shadow over Julius's crumpled hands as he worked over my mother's wedding dress to fit me even then I guess I must have known I wouldn't go through with it; in 2008 in a corner of the NICU waiting room at Strong Hospital in Rochester NY while my husband and I waited for someone to come out and tell us whether or not our newborn son would live or not the red-orange switch light flickered like a tiny tongue of fire, one of many ubiquitous tiny lights, I suppose, burning in the myriad dark places where people must wait for whatever comes.

Self-Portrait Part I

I like rag dolls for their fortitude; if only we could all be made of such forgiving stuff.

I like a chicken fried steak and sausage gravy supper made from seitan; I would like it even better if I could order it in a roadside diner, but this will never happen.

I like Kung Fu movies and Hong Kong action films, especially those starring Michelle Yeoh or Angela Mao, or Do-yeon Jeon as these women are beautiful, patient, merciful and badass, four things to which I have always aspired, with varying degrees of success.

Fairy tales, I like those, the original ones, written by Jacob and Wilhelm Grimm; why we pretty them up for kids anymore is beyond me, as a little bit of fear is good for the soul, or so I've always believed.

I like Dodo birds. Not the fat overfed ones in Victorian sketches, but the ones that the Dutch vice-admiral Wybrand Van Warwijck first wrote about, whose species only enjoyed a 72 year run; once discovered by humans, we made short work of them, and for this I am profoundly sorry.

Graveyards, I like those (underground records of fashion), and stick-shift cars and ten-year-old Subarus and Airstream travel trailers and Blue Heeler dogs and beat up old beach cruiser bicycles; I like all these for all the obvious reasons.

Tumbleweeds, I like these because they are also called *windwitches,* and they make me feel lonesome,

and I'm often inspired by inchworms, inexhaustible intrepid measurers of the infinite; yes, I really like inchworms a lot.

I like the work of Rambo the New Zealand octographer because she can always capture a sense of wonder on the faces of her subjects,

and along those lines, I also like box jellyfish with their top-
lensed eye always pointing upward, scanning for
mangrove canopies that signal food and shelter.

I like onions of all types, but especially Red Zeppelins and Mayan
Sweets; I like them because they manage to take on color
despite their dark beginnings; I like it that you can peel
away layer after layer until finally there is nothing left but
the white silence that lives deep within.

Self-Portrait Part II

I don't like potluck dinners, other people's kids, or eating off of paper plates.

I don't like wearing socks or making plans, and I hate it when automatic doors won't open for me, which, for whatever reason, seems to happen a lot.

I don't like driving in heavy traffic, those mechanical shoals of humanity, always moving toward the sketchy destinations of noplace else.

I don't like the Jew's Harp someone gave my son. I don't like it because the music is annoying and because calling it a "Jew's Harp" makes me uncomfortable, even though the rabbi who lives across the street told me it was fine, and that I shouldn't give it another thought.

Facetime, Skype and talking on telephones of any sort; I don't like these things because they cause me to exist in two places at once, sort of, which makes me a little bit nervous.

I don't like hostile, socioeconomically-politically-inclined intellectual voluptuaries who exist in perpetual states of outrage because they make me feel stupid and simple and uninformed every time I try to participate in "The Conversation."

I don't like the indecipherable tap code of rainwater on my Norfolk Tides ballcap hatbrim, or the runic expressions of earthworms in the Virginia Beach Community Garden vermicomposted soil, because these are constant reminders that there are things in life I will never understand, no matter how hard I try.

I don't like inland palm trees, urban seagulls or mistletoe that flowers in spring, as these things confuse my sense of logic and order.

I don't like the leopard print *Boob Buddy* bra holster someone gave me for my .38, which I never carry around with me anyway, as I don't really like the .38 either. And I would like to think that I'd hold a a home invader hostage, maybe even offer him or her a cup of coffee, until help arrived, but I've been around long enough to know that there's a killer napping within of each of us; I don't care for that napper stirring in the shadows of my being.

I don't like it when the hospital ship USS Comfort and the carrier-based Sea Angels are in port, because in my mind this means that there is that much more unattended suffering in the world.

I don't like standing on Pier Number 10 at Naval Station Norfolk, waiting for the awful assault ship USS Kearsarge to come home from its horrible mission; I want to go invisible, I want to die of embarrassment, but I must remain visible and alive because someone on that ship who loves me a lot will be looking for me soon.

Tarquinian Rag Doll

The little Tarquinian rag doll named *Camilla*
will fit in just fine with the other
Italian rag dolls on my daughter's bed
back home: Jacqueline, the peasant girl
from Caltagirone, scooped up and held close
when the named and unnamed storms shake the house;
Annabelle, the dancer from Napoli, with her two puffy
pointe shoes, hauled along to rehearsal after rehearsal
in the purple and red floral Vera Bradly ballet bag.
And Isobel from Agrigento, in her tee-shirt and denim jumper,
the tree-climbing, bike-riding buddy, always
slightly unkempt. All day, while my daughter
goes to school they remain carefully tucked
inside their shoebox beds under tiny handmade quilts
my mother stitched, resting amid picture books
and bins of pink legos. Camilla, I'm sure,
will find her place. It's noon here in Italy,
and the shopkeeper's radio picks up the
Polish *Hejnal Mariachi (St. Mary's Dawn)*,
a daily broadcast from almost one thousand miles away.
Camilla's peach-colored yarn pigtails,
her green and yellow flower printed-dress;
someday I'll tell my daughter about the young
Polish mother on the outskirts of Krakow
who approached my parents and begged them
to take her little girl home with them,
for what she imagined would be a much better life.

Fragment of the Tomb of Hunting and Fishing

—(a poem written on a post card)

By the time you get this,
I will have already returned
home, the same person I was
before I left, only more so.
At the exact moment this arrives,
you will likely be elbow deep
in someone's else's misery,
surgeon's loupes illuminating
a body gone wrong. The Etruscan
tomb painters understood
that our place in this world is small;
good to remember that even
the occasional dark ocean
offers plenty of elusive, living stuff,
enough to sustain us for a good long time.

Well

Well what?

What about chickens, will there be chickens?

Oh yes, lots of chickens, Leghorns and Winnebagos and Rhode Island Reds, and Buff Orpingtons, to name a few, and you won't have to eat them, you can just kick back in your rocker and run your bare feet through their feathers.

Okay. That sounds nice, that sounds really nice, but how about a goat? We might need a goat, too.

Yep, there's already a goat. Her name is Lily, and she's fifteen years old. Which is kind of old for a goat, but there you have it.

Does she keep the grass trimmed?

She keeps the grass trimmed.

Does she eat the trash?

Only the paper, cardboard and aluminum cans.

Will she buck the trolls off of the bridge?

We don't have a bridge.

Do we have trolls?

Not sure about the trolls.

We should consider trolls.

A troll might be nice.

We could get an ugly one.

An unhelpful one.

An unfriendly one….

To mix things up a bit….

To keep us from crossing the bridge!

The one that we don't have!

What about the peepers for the swamp?

Only in spring.

But it's never spring….how about horses?

Oh no, horses would break our hearts.

I was thinking about oxen.

Are there oxen anymore? Anywhere?

I don't know, but I like to think about them and I like to say oxen: oxen.

Oxen.

Oxen.

Oxen.

Oxen.

Oxen.

Maybe a peacock to wander around the place.

Isn't there some significance, sexual or otherwise, associated with peacocks?

Is there?

Maybe. I'm not sure. I think so. I don't know.

I don't either.

It's too risky.

Agreed. No peacock.

We'll need a good well.

I guess we'll need that first. Something to draw from. When all else fails.

All else won't fail.

I certainly hope not.

All else never fails.

Well?

Well.

Well.

[…]

Alright, then.

I Arrive at this Moment and Now What?

It's all happened so fast, the way a black rat snake pursues its prey
through a field of green zebras;

it's been a little bit insidious, the way that passports lost
to pickpockets give birth to secret, similar, double
identities whose life paths will not likely cross again;

there've been plenty of slippery slopes, surprising
descents down gin-greased streets, through which I
barrelassed euphorically, an overgrown running child
following the rolling ball.

Often, the simultaneous sense of disappointment and wonder, the
kind that time travelers who whoosh through electrically-
charged wormholes realize, since they rarely arrive in the
precise moments they'd initially imagined;

always, a telekinetic quality is present, as an invisible cavernous
yawn traveling the globe like a renegade virus, passing
from one unwary person to the next that vacuous library
of half-said human stuff, until entire continents finally go
unconscious.

And today, having just arrived in Italy once again, there comes
from nowhere the song of the same mixed-up night
rooster who has stalked me for years;

crowing at odd hours of the night and well into the day, in a
twenty-four-hour romance analog of awakening he says:

*pay attention already, you have already lost a day just getting here
and you don't even know how many days there are left to
lose, now do you…?*

A Palpable Sense of Lollygagging

(Opulent marble chandeliers); the spiritual
fortification of the notoriously unforgiving
sober reality of marketable testimonials
(something akin to baseball cap five o'clock shadow
seashell windchimes). Merciless statistic star-shredded
culture luminary. A pointless pencil kickstart,
a viral buzz, a resplendent spoof lobby
in the balmy breezeby (he checks his look
in the robot's reflection, and then she does it, too);
idiosyncratic pudding redemptive,
hamfist cellmate, hackneyed atonement,
cute recluse host, gregarious amen.

She Crab Soup

I'll have a beaker of ice-cubed
essence of something awesome
centrifuged at 4,700 rotations per minute
by a molecular mixologist for exactly
ten lunic millimoments. Maybe top it off,
as they say, with *a cool nose of mint.*
(Oh futuristic sonic homogenizer!)
(Oh ultrasonic sound wave emulsifier!)
(Oh rotary evaporation extraction!)
Love the inaugural nitro popcorn
pairing of protonic corncobs, jalapeñocarbic
cayenne, and blastochardonnay. And gimme
some of that spectroplasmic sherry and roe,
and, please, a bit of that irridated She Crab Soup.

Aubade

Morning of the day of the imminent
  oblivion potluck supper.
Morning of the cat's eye marble hailstorm,
  the scattershot almanac's most recent misprediction.
Morning of the off-center sunrise
  that roasted the Eastside birds, made skeletons
  of all the best trees, and burned like prayer beads
  in the dark pockets of public enemies.
Sandman Boulevard seasick Cape May-Lewes ferry boat morning
  of the downhome heading-back-to-Dixie road trip.
Acme morning, Fuller Brush and Amway morning.
Morning of naked people stepping in and and out of showers.
Morning of airzooka laughter cannonballs and unfamiliar seagulls.
Megladon memory and birdnapped peacock morning.
Unsuccessful codecrack morning of silver slime trail ciphers
  left by locomoting mollusks.
Badass pelican morning of the working lighthouse.
Morning of massive, imaginary meteors hurtling toward Earth,
  deflected at the last dramatic second.
Low breathy morning of mechanical hearts and electric brains
  (a metric assload of these) coolly pursuing
  the calming shade of invisible sideswiping sunspots.

Free Clean Dirt Wanted

Thimble Shoal Channel Tunnel Roth Bridge Dreamland Trailer Park
(shitsuck truck peace token cigarette shop). Snallygaster
salty oysters redbud fish fry U.S. Highway 13.
Kudzu poultry shorebird baseball (Dover military
decedent affairs), crude oil placard 1267, Hope
Creek nuclear cooling towers. All new sushi tex mex
disco nightclub: if you lived here you would be home.

Seminomad Prayer Termite

Despite its trifling size,
the doll hacks at a promising new soup
for a troubled iguana. Pawns
on many lucrative delinquents
ache on the vertigo of estrus.
Most flappers have not camouflaged
enough tranquilizers to rival them.
In an efflux to dodge and style their red ink,
some delinquentmarvels are beginning to shovel
ancillary string beans tossed to their weasels.
Proteus's termite, which eludes prayers
to riddle discoveries about a plastid
back to dachshunds (after they have been
scrambled), incants a prime equity.
When one of Proteus's prayers is tripled,
sermon flusters atomize the edible cobalt dandy
it creates, which swaddles wireless swaggers
through the barbershop, talking another cartwheel,
worn as a starveling parole, or echoed
just under the swoosh. That, in turn,
can unlatch discoveries to a seminomad paragrapher
or squiggle icons to a dachshund
via the inspector. Thus, it idolizes easy
to mock a plastid tripling his prayers
at the right temperature, to spank adverse
ribosomes with other delinquents,
and so on.

M. Jeanne Skvarla was born in Austin, Texas and grew up in Norman, Oklahoma. She studied English Literature and Philosophy at Oklahoma State University, and later earned her M.F.A. in Poetry from the University of Massachusetts at Amherst. She has worked as a pizza shop manager, paramedic, accountant, English teacher, farrier, editor, DNA lab autoclave operator and botanical micrographer at various places in Oklahoma, New England and Western New York. She is an active member of the Poetry Society of Virginia, and her poems have appeared in such journals as *College English, Rattle*, and *Poetry East.* She currently lives in Virginia Beach, VA. This is her first collection of poetry.

www.ingramcontent.com/pod-product-compliance
Lightning Source LLC
Chambersburg PA
CBHW070550090426
42735CB00013B/3143
9781635341508